Conten

SHAPE STORIES

1. Use the questions on each worksheet to stimulate pre-writing discussions. You may choose to write vocabulary words on the chalkboard for the students to use as they write their stories.

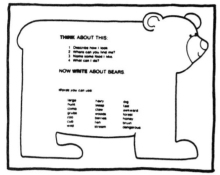
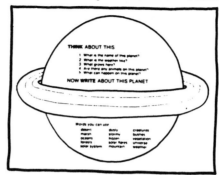
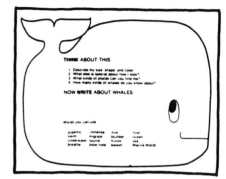
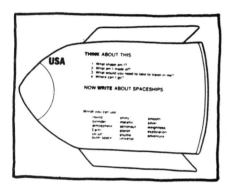
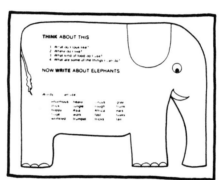
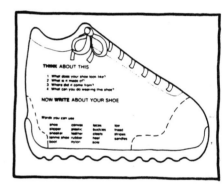

2. Make writing paper by using the basic shape on the worksheet as a template. Cut out the shape. Lay it onto writing paper and trace around it. Cut out as many sheets as you need.

3. Make a cover for the completed stories by tracing the shape onto a piece of construction paper. Trace, cut out, and staple the cover together with the stories the children have written. Select a child to decorate the cover.

   Place it in your classroom library to be enjoyed again and again.

Note
Use an encyclopedia or nonfiction book to collect facts about each writing topic.

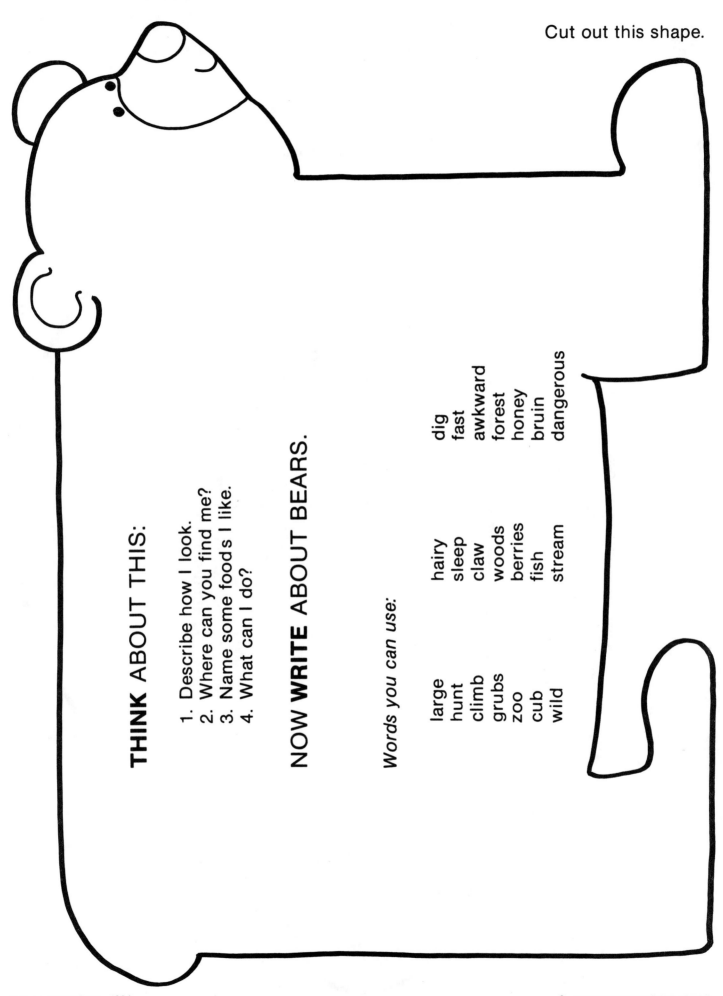

Cut out this shape.

THINK ABOUT THIS:

1. Describe how I look.
2. Where can you find me?
3. Name some foods I like.
4. What can I do?

NOW **WRITE** ABOUT BEARS.

Words you can use:

large	hairy	dig
hunt	sleep	fast
climb	claw	awkward
grubs	woods	forest
zoo	berries	honey
cub	fish	bruin
wild	stream	dangerous

Cut out this shape.

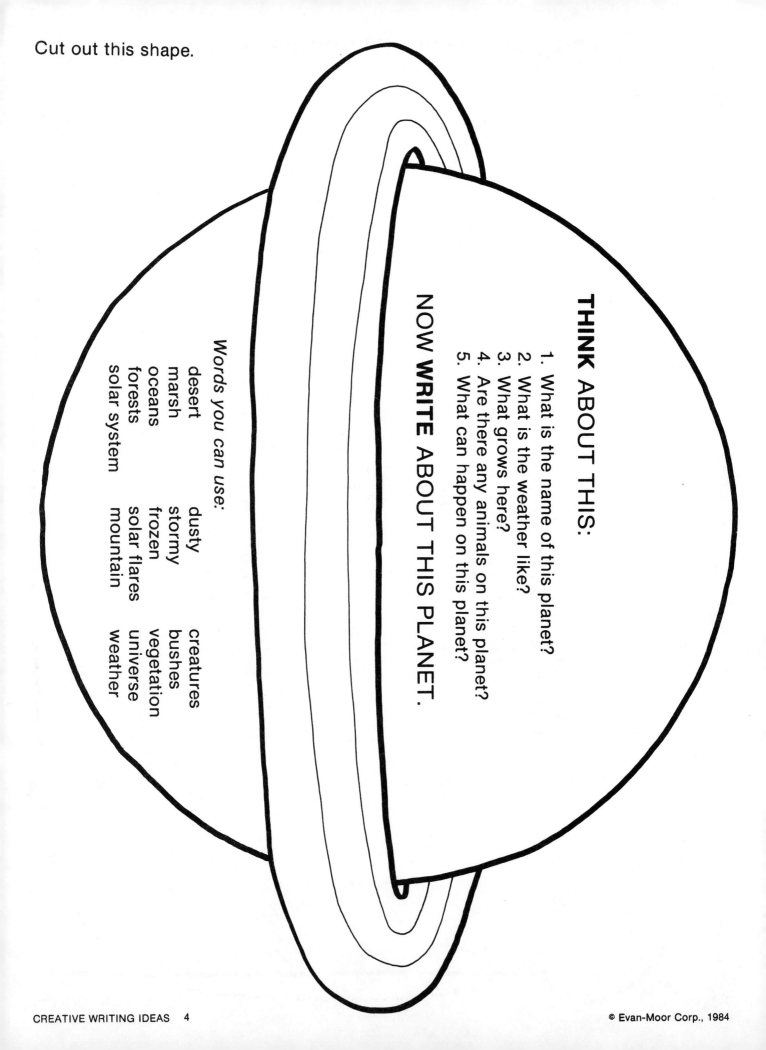

THINK ABOUT THIS:

1. What is the name of this planet?
2. What is the weather like?
3. What grows here?
4. Are there any animals on this planet?
5. What can happen on this planet?

NOW **WRITE ABOUT THIS PLANET.**

Words you can use:

desert	dusty	creatures
marsh	stormy	bushes
oceans	frozen	vegetation
forests	solar flares	universe
solar system	mountain	weather

THINK ABOUT THIS:

1. Describe my size, shape, and color.
2. What else is special about how I look?
3. What kinds of places can you find me?
4. How many kinds of whales do you know about?

NOW **WRITE** ABOUT WHALES.

Words you can use:

gigantic	immense	dive	float
swim	migrate	blubber	ocean
underwater	sound	flukes	sea
breathe	blow hole	baleen	Marine World

Cut out this shape.

Cut out this shape.

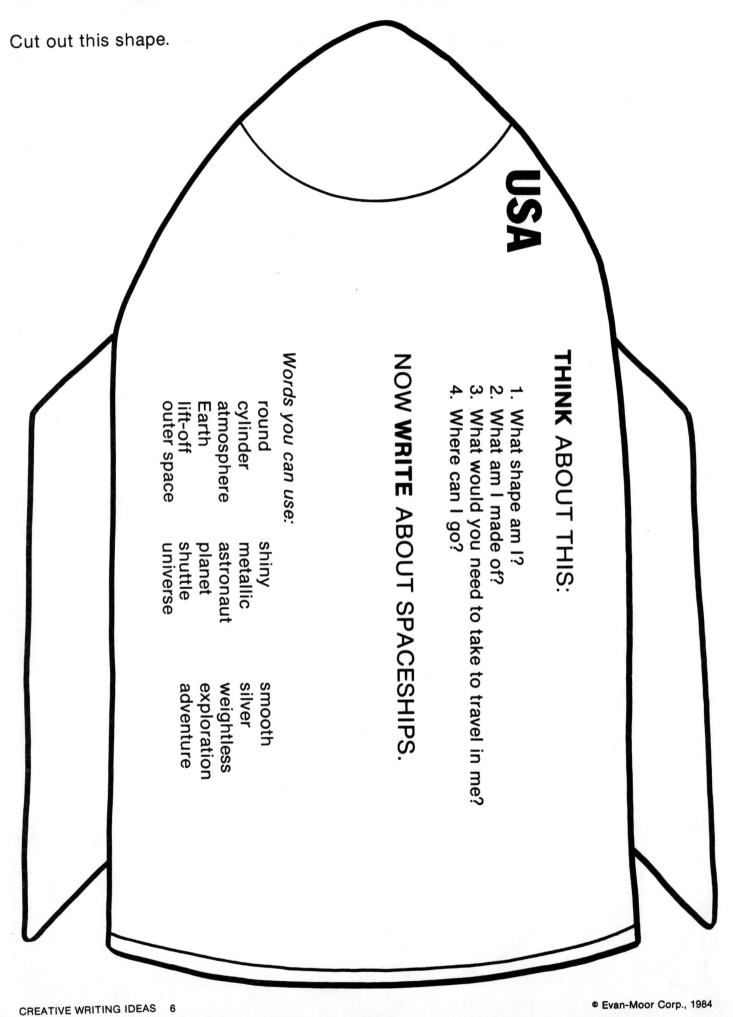

USA

THINK ABOUT THIS:

1. What shape am I?
2. What am I made of?
3. What would you need to take to travel in me?
4. Where can I go?

NOW **WRITE** ABOUT SPACESHIPS.

Words you can use:

round	shiny	smooth
cylinder	metallic	silver
atmosphere	astronaut	weightless
Earth	planet	exploration
lift-off	shuttle	adventure
outer space	universe	

THINK ABOUT THIS:

1. What do I look like?
2. Where do I live?
3. What kinds of food do I use?
4. What are some of the things I can do?

NOW **WRITE** ABOUT ELEPHANTS.

Words you can use:

enormous	heavy	gray
thick	jungle	trunk
floppy	Asia	ears
huge	work	circus
wrinkled	trumpet	rough
		Africa
		fast
		tricks
		tusks
		tail

Cut out this shape.

Cut out this shape.

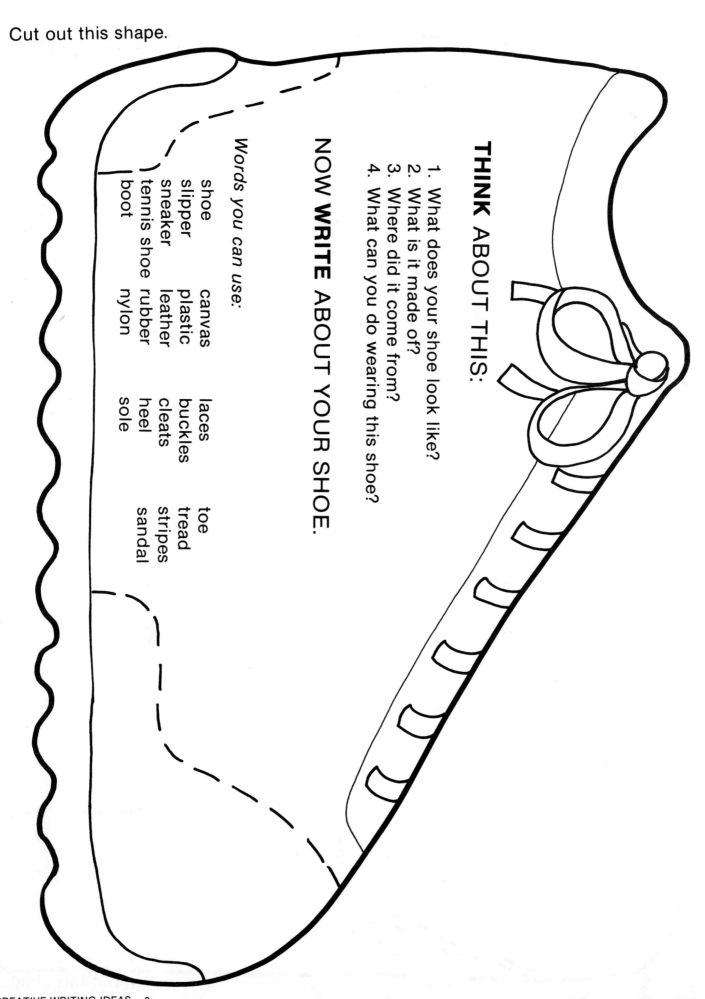

THINK ABOUT THIS:

1. What does your shoe look like?
2. What is it made of?
3. Where did it come from?
4. What can you do wearing this shoe?

NOW **WRITE** ABOUT YOUR SHOE.

Words you can use:

shoe	canvas	laces	toe
slipper	plastic	buckles	tread
sneaker	leather	cleats	stripes
tennis shoe	rubber	heel	sandal
boot	nylon	sole	

Draw and Write

The drawing steps and questions provided on each worksheet are designed to stimulate the student's imagination and to serve as a springboard to writing a story.

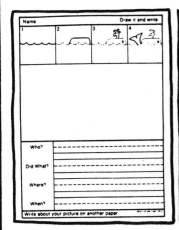  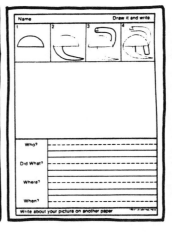 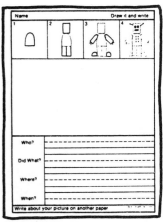

1. Student follows steps to complete a drawing. Background details are added to the drawing.

2. The questions at the bottom of the page are answered as a first step in writing the story.

3. Next the student takes a sheet of writing paper and, using the previous step, creates a short story about the drawing.

You may create a class book by having students paste the drawing and the finished story to a sheet of construction paper. Then staple all papers together and add a construction paper cover.

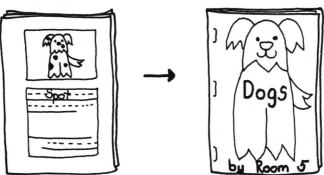

Name			Draw it and write.

1	2	3	4

Who?

Did What?

Where?

When?

Write about your picture on another paper.

CREATIVE WRITING IDEAS

Draw it and write.

1

2

3

4

Who?

Did What?

Where?

When?

Write about your picture on another paper.

Draw it and write.

| 1 | 2 | 3 | 4 |

Who?

- -

Did What?

- -

Where?

- -

When?

- -

Name	Draw it and write.

1	2	3	4

Who?

Did What?

Where?

When?

Write about your picture on another paper.

RIDDLES!

Prepare students for riddle writing by setting up questions they can think about to guide them in the actual writing process.

Brown Bag Riddles—riddles about objects

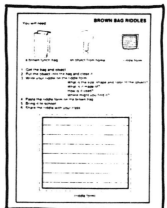

What is its size?
What is its shape?
What color is it?
What is it made of?
How is it used?
Where might you find it?

In My Lunch Box—riddles about food

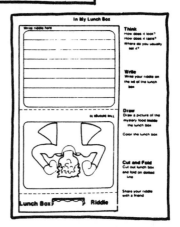

What does it look like?
How does it taste?
How does it smell?
When do you usually eat it?

Animal Pop-ups—riddles about animals

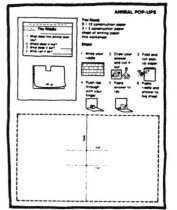

What is its physical appearance?
Where does it live?
What does it eat?
What can it do?
Does it make a sound?
Does Man use it in any way?

Can You Guess Who I Am?—riddles about people

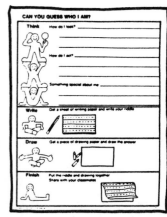

How does this person look?
Describe the behavior of this person or tell an activity he/she can do.
What is unique (special) about this person?
When and where did this person live? (for historical figures)

Some people you can write riddles about are:

yourself	character from a story
classmates	someone from history
teacher	sports figure
someone in your family	
someone from the movies or TV	

BROWN BAG RIDDLES

You will need:

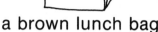
a brown lunch bag

an object from home

riddle form

1. Get the bag and object.
2. Put the object into the bag and close it.
3. Write your riddle on the riddle form.

>   What is the size, shape, and color of the object?
>   What is it made of?
>   How is it used?
>   Where might you find it?

4. Paste the riddle form on the brown bag.
5. Bring it to school.
6. Share the riddle with your class.

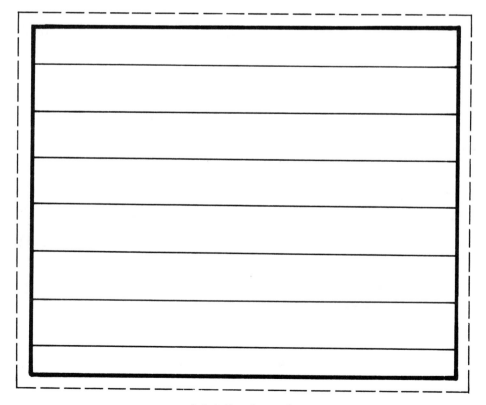

(riddle form)

In My Lunch Box

Write riddle here.

This belongs to

Lunch Box **Riddle**

Think
How does it look?
How does it taste?
Where do you usually eat it?

Write
Write your riddle on the lid of the lunch box.

Draw
Draw a picture of the mystery food **inside** the lunch box.

Color the lunch box.

Cut and Fold
Cut out lunch box and fold on dotted line.

Share your riddle with a friend.

ANIMAL POP-UPS

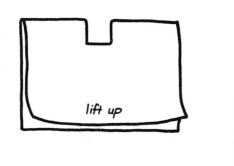

The Riddle

1. What does this animal look like?
2. Where does it live?
3. What does it eat?
4. What can it do?

lift up

You Need:
9 × 12 construction paper
3 × 3 white construction paper
sheet of writing paper
this worksheet

Steps:

1. Write your riddle.

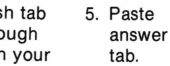

2. Draw your answer and cut it out.

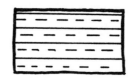

3. Fold and cut pop-up paper.

4. Push tab through with your finger.

5. Paste answer to tab.

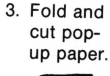

6. Paste riddle and answer to big sheet.

fold

cut

cut

CAN YOU GUESS WHO I AM?

Think

How do I look? _____

_____

_____

How do I act? _____

_____

_____

Something special about me: _____

_____

Write   Get a sheet of writing paper and write your riddle.

Draw   Get a piece of drawing paper and draw the answer.

Finish   Put the riddle and drawing together.
Share with your classmates.

SEQUENCE AND WRITE

The directions are the same for each "sequence and write" worksheet.

1. Reproduce the worksheet.

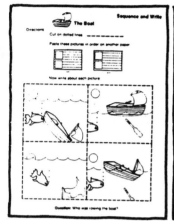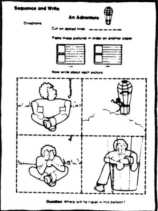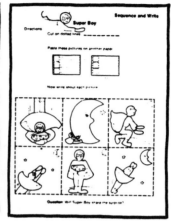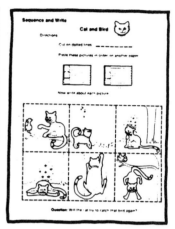

2. Student cuts the pictures apart and pastes them in order down the side of a sheet of writing paper.

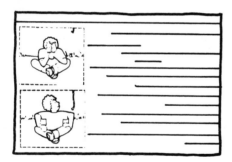

Use the back or a second sheet of paper.

3. Students write a paragraph about each picture to create a complete story.

You will have better results if you allow time for oral discussion of what is happening in each picture before students begin to write.

 **The Boat**

Directions:

Cut on dotted lines. ▬ ▬ ▬ ▬ ▬ ▬ ▬ ▬

Paste these pictures in order on another paper.

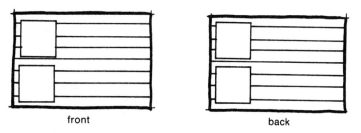

front   back

Now write about each picture.

Question: Who was rowing the boat?

Sequence and Write

An Adventure

Directions:

Cut on dotted lines. — — — — —

Paste these pictures in order on another paper.

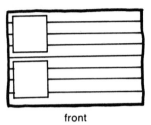 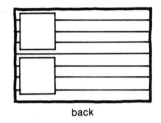

front   back

Now write about each picture.

Question: Where will he travel in this balloon?

Super Boy

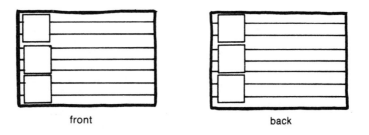

Directions:

Cut on dotted lines. ▬ ▬ ▬ ▬ ▬ ▬ ▬

Paste these pictures on another paper.

front   back

Now write about each picture.

Question: Will Super Boy share the surprise?

Sequence and Write

Cat and Bird

Directions:

Cut on dotted lines. ___ ___ ___ ___

Paste these pictures in order on another paper.

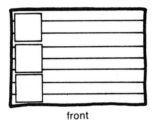 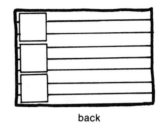

front   back

Now write about each picture.

Question: Will the cat try to catch that bird again?

FILL IN THE MISSING WORDS

SENTENCES:

Students practice using adjectives and verbs in this activity. They select two words to describe the animal named; then tell what the animal is doing.

Example:

A <u>tall</u>, <u>spotted</u> giraffe <u>nibbled leaves from a tree</u>.
That <u>small</u>, <u>angry</u> monkey <u>chattered loudly</u>.

ALLITERATIVE PHRASES:

Children practice adjectives and nouns by completing phrases containing "group" words. They provide a description and noun each beginning with the same letter or sound as the "group" word given.

Example:

a bunch of <u>busy</u> <u>boys</u>
a bunch of <u>barefoot</u> <u>boxers</u>
a bunch of <u>beautiful</u> <u>blossoms</u>

a group of <u>grumpy</u> <u>grown-ups</u>
a mob of <u>merry</u> <u>monkeys</u>
a bevy of <u>blue</u> <u>butterflies</u>

SHORT STORIES:

A short story is provided. Children fill in the blanks choosing words from the Word Bank provided at the bottom of the page or making up their own answers.

Example:

BANG! went the starting gun. The <u>exciting</u> race had begun. <u>Varoom</u> went the motors of the <u>powerful, new</u> racing cars.

27

A TRIP TO THE ZOO

Describe each animal and tell what it is doing.

A _____ , _____ zebra _____

_____ .

That _____ , _____ elephant _____

_____ .

Some _____ , _____ giraffes _____

_____ .

The _____ , _____ boa constrictor _____

_____ .

Two _____ , _____ monkeys _____

_____ .

The _____ , _____ ostrich _____

_____ .

Will that _____ , _____ crocodile _____

_____ ?

Can a _____ , _____ gorilla _____

_____ ?

A SHEET OF SILLY SAYINGS

Choose a describing word and a naming word that begin with the same sound as the underlined word.

Example: a bunch of ___*bouncing babies*___

1. a **bunch** of _____

2. a **gang** of _____

3. a **flock** of _____

4. a **mob** of _____

5. a **group** of _____

6. a **herd** of _____

7. a **crowd** of _____

8. a **throng** of _____

9. a **gathering** of _____

10. a **mass** of _____

The Race

Fill in the blanks to create an exciting story about race cars.

BANG! went the starting gun. The _____

race had begun . _____ went the motors of the

_____ , _____ racing cars.

Number 7 _____ around a _____ curve.

Down the _____ track _____ the cars.

Number 19 was ready to pass when _____ his

tire went flat! Too bad Number 19!   Number 7 _____

over the finish line to win the _____ race.

_____ went the crowd. Number 7 felt very

_____ . Number 19 went _____

back to the pit. Maybe next time he would be the winner.

Word Box
Use these words or make up answers of your own.

exciting	dusty	smooth	chug-chug
powerful	sped	slowly	muddy
roared	proud	thrilling	zoomed
sadly	shiny	hurrah	plop
hiss	flat	hummm	tired
championship	hurried	suddenly	dangerous
slick	steep	excited	suddenly

   CREATIVE WRITING IDEAS

Beth and Tabby

This story is missing all the sound words.
Fill in the blanks to create an exciting story about Beth and Tabby.

_____ went the alarm clock. Beth leaped out of bed.

_____ went her blankets onto the floor. _____

went her feet. She heard a _____ , _____ ,

_____ sound outside. Her bedroom slippers went _____

as she hurried to the window. Hailstones were _____ all

around. _____ , _____ went the chunks of

ice on the roofs of cars and houses.

_____ ! _____ ! _____ ! There

was a noise at the back door. Poor Tabby had been left outside.   Beth

hurried to let her cat in. As Beth slammed the door with a _____ ,

Tabby jumped up and began licking her face. _____ !

Word Box
Use these words or make up answers of your own.
You may add endings to these words. Use a word more than once if
you wish.

bang	creak	plop	swish
crash	click	splat	hum
clunk	gurgle	hiss	buzz
pow	blub-blub	crunch	scratch
meow	purr	tick-tock	boom
flip-flop	rattle	slurp	pitter-pat

   • EVAN-MOOR CORP., 1984

This unit contains twelve story starters ready to motivate students to write.

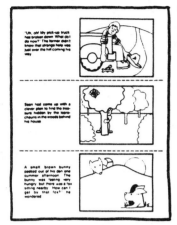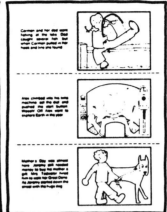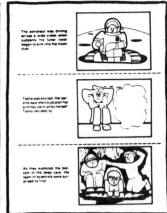

METHOD I:

One story starter is written on the board. Students copy the story starter on their own paper and complete the story.

METHOD II:

A page of story starters is reproduced. Cut the sections apart. Children paste one story starter to the top of writing paper and complete the story.

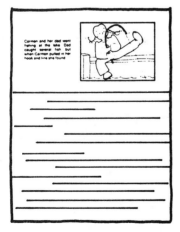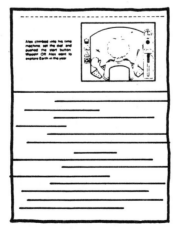

Printed story starters and writing paper can be placed in a center for free time or extra writing experiences. They may also be used as homework activities.

"Uh, oh! My pick-up truck has broken down. What do I do now?" The farmer didn't know that strange help was just over the hill coming his way.

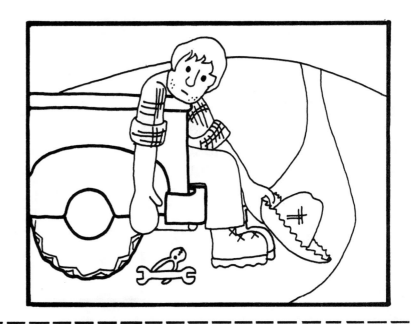

Sean had come up with a clever plan to find the treasure hidden by the leprechauns in the woods behind his house.

A small brown bunny peeked out of his den one summer afternoon. The bunny was feeling very hungry, but there was a fox sitting nearby. "How can I get by that fox?" he wondered.

My little brother is so care-less. Monday he lost his gloves. Yesterday he lost his cap. Mom is very upset because today he lost . . .

Aunt Ethel sent George a plant for his birthday. George woke up in the mid-dle of the night and heard the plant say . . .

It was a dark, cold morning. It had been snowing since late last night. When Sal walked out the front door, he saw something unusual.

Carmen and her dad went fishing at the lake. Dad caught several fish, but when Carmen pulled in her hook and line she found . . .

Alex climbed into his time machine, set the dial, and pushed the start button. Woosh! Off Alex went to explore Earth in the year . . .

Mother's Day was almost here. Jeremy still needed money to buy his mother a gift. Mrs. Todwater hired him to walk her Great Dane. As Jeremy started down the street with the huge dog, . . .

The astronaut was driving across a wide crater when suddenly his lunar rover began to sink into the moon dust.

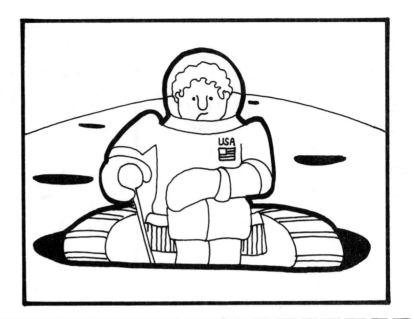

Tasha was excited. Her parents said she could plan her birthday party all by herself. Tasha decided to . . .

As they explored the bottom of the deep cave, the team of scientists were surprised to find . . .

CARTOONS

Sample questions for pre-writing discussions are given with each set of directions. Write students' ideas on the chalkboard.

Dreams

Discuss: Have you ever had a _____ dream?

scary   funny   unusual   exciting   strange

What was your most favorite dream?
Have you ever had a dream that seemed real?

Directions:
Students are to write a paragraph describing the character's dream using the space provided.

At The Pond

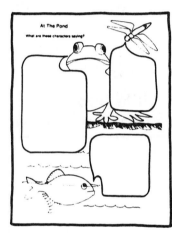

Discuss: What could be happening at the pond?
How would you describe frog's expression?
            fish's
            dragonfly's
Why might he feel this way?
What do you think he is saying?

Directions:
Children write what they think each character might be saying.
Encourage children to try to create a conversation that tells a story.

The Runner

Discuss: Why is this character running?
   (toward what? away from what?)
How is the runner feeling?
What might happen while he/she is running?

Box 1—WHO are you?
Box 2 ⎰WHERE and WHY are you
Box 3 ⎱running?
Box 4—WHAT finally happens?

Directions:
Students fill in the speaking bubbles using the first person.
They add clothing and a background appropriate to their story.

Cartoon Cut-ups

Discuss: What kinds of problems might penguins have? Think about how each penguin looks. What could be causing these expressions and actions? What could each penguin be saying?

Directions:

Fold large, white paper into 6 boxes.

Cut penguins out and organize them in an order that suggests a story.

Draw a speech bubble in each box.

Write what each penguin is saying each time. Try to make it tell a story.

A Little Book

Discuss: Brainstorm with your class to develop a list of possible topics on which to write.

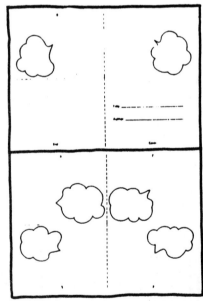

What type of characters could be in your story?

What might happen to this character? (Limit the number of problems.)

What kind of pictures can you make to show what is happening?

What might the characters say to tell your story?

Setting a theme such as **Fortunately . . . Unfortunately, Happily . . .Unhappily, Then . . . Now,** or **Before . . . After** can help children who are not ready to create a complete story.

Directions:

Reproduce the two "little book" pages for each student. Fold on the dotted lines. Staple the pages in order.

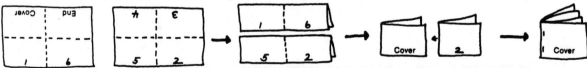

Students draw their pictures, then write the conversations in the speech bubbles.

What are you dreaming about?

At The Pond

What are these characters saying?

Teacher: Provide large paper, scissors, paste and
pencils for this activity.

CARTOON CUT-UPS

1. Fold your big paper into six boxes.

2. Cut out the penguins and arrange them in
   the boxes. Paste them.

3. Draw a 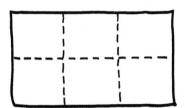 by each penguin. Write
   what he is saying in the bubble.

4. Draw the background for each picture.

The Runner   Fill in the bubbles.

1.

2.

3.

4.

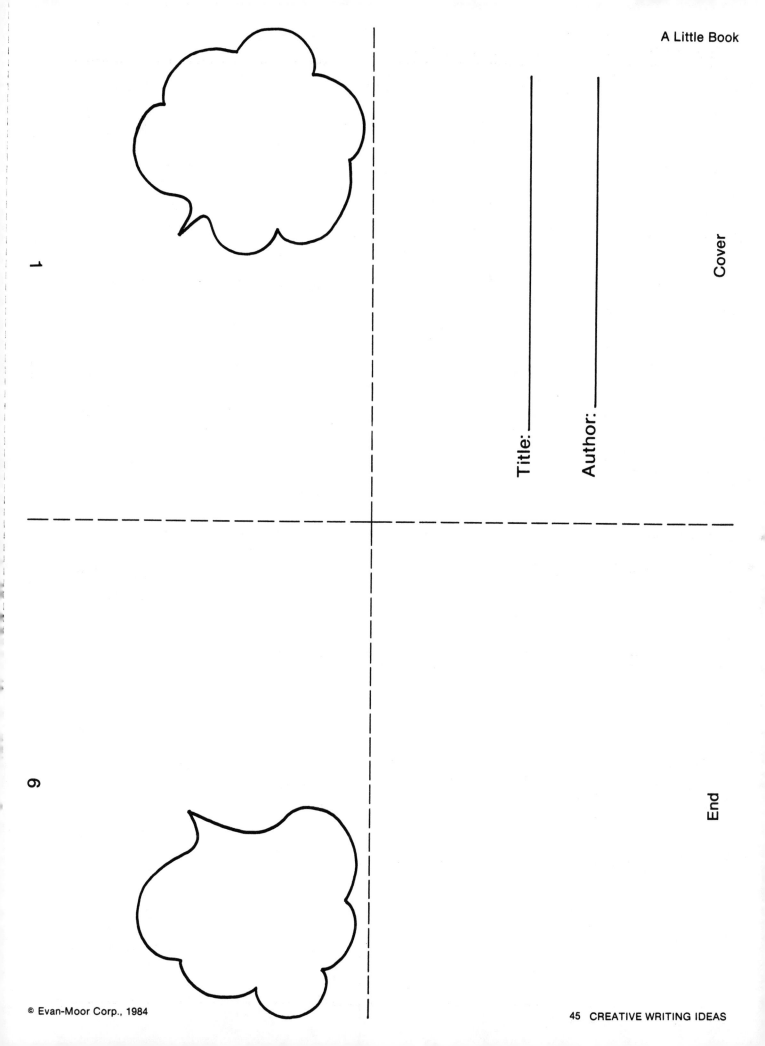

Cover

Title: _____

Author: _____

1

6

End

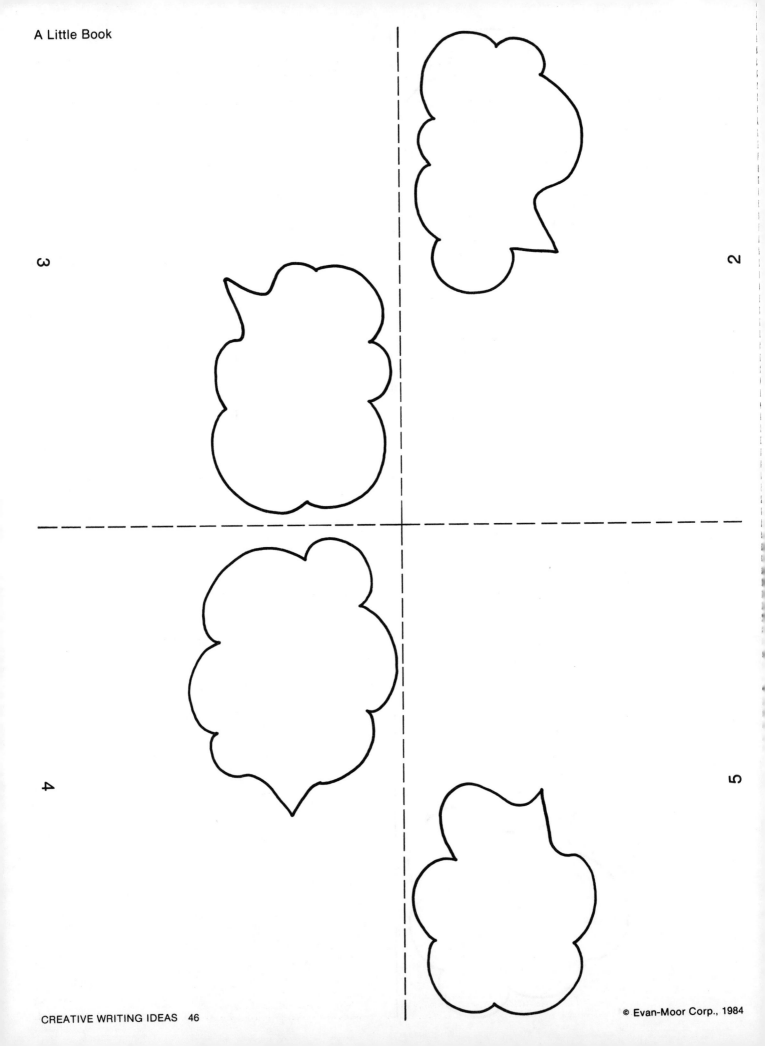

3

2

4

5

DESCRIPTIVE PARAGRAPHS

Practice by doing oral descriptions using objects around the classroom, pictures from magazines, the children in the class, etc. Provide questions and word lists as a guide to help get reluctant writers started.

Describing Objects:

What does the object look like? (color, size, shape, texture)
What other characteristics does it have? (taste, smell, sound)
How is it used?
Where can you find it?

Children practice writing descriptions of objects using the worksheets provided in this section.

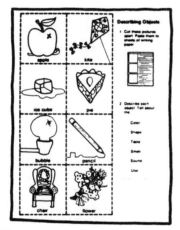

Describing Feelings:

What are some of the feelings people experience? (happy, sad, disappointed, embarrassed, excited)
What experiences can cause these feelings?
Have you ever felt _____ ? What did you do?

Children practice writing descriptions of feelings using the worksheets provided in this section.

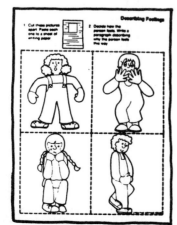
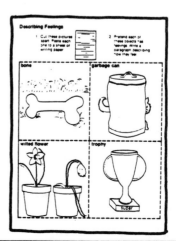

Describing Places:

Where is this place located?
What are its physical characteristics?
Does it contain any special characteristics?

Children practice writing descriptions of places
using the worksheet provided in this section.

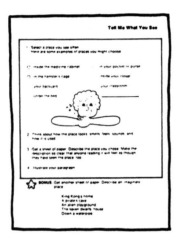

Describing People:

How does the person look? (hair, eye color, skin, size, age)
How does this person usually act?
What is special about this person?
What can this person do best?

Children practice writing descriptions of people
using the worksheet provided in this section.

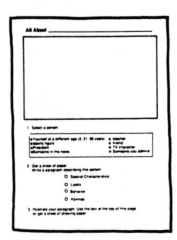

apple

kite

ice cube

pie

bubble

pencil

chair

flowers

Describing Objects

1. Cut these pictures apart. Paste them to sheets of writing paper.

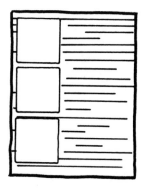

2. Describe each object. Tell about the:

   Color

   Shape

   Taste

   Smell

   Sound

   Use

What Can It Be?

Draw an imaginary object. Choose one of these, or create one of
your own:

A robot with an unusual talent

An underwater apartment house for squid

A machine to make peanut butter and jelly sandwiches

A burglar-proof piggy bank

Get a sheet of paper. Write a paragraph describing the object
and how to use it.

Describing Feelings

1. Cut these pictures apart. Paste each one to a sheet of writing paper.

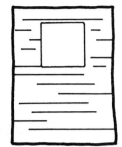

2. Decide how the person feels. Write a paragraph describing why the person feels this way.

51

Describing Feelings

1. Cut these pictures apart. Paste each one to a sheet of writing paper.

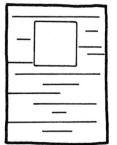

2. Pretend each of these objects has feelings. Write a paragraph describing how they feel.

bone

garbage can

wilted flower

trophy

super

Tell Me What You See

1. Select a place you see often.
   Here are some examples of places you might choose:

   ○ inside the medicine cabinet ○ in your pocket or purse

   ○ in the hamster's cage ○ inside your closet

   ○ your backyard ○ your classroom

   ○ under the bed ○ _____
   other

2. Think about how the place looks, smells, feels, sounds, and how it is used.

3. Get a sheet of paper. Describe the place you chose. Make the description so clear that anyone reading it will feel as though they have seen the place too.

4. Illustrate your paragraph.

 BONUS: Get another sheet of paper. Describe an imaginary place.

- King Kong's home
- a pirate's cave
- an alien playground
- the seven dwarfs' house
- down a waterpipe

All About _____

```



```

1. Select a person:

- yourself at a different age (2, 21, 90 years)
- sports figure
- President
- someone in the news
- teacher
- friend
- TV character
- someone you admire

2. Get a sheet of paper.
   Write a paragraph describing this person.

   O Special Characteristics

   O Looks

   O Behavior

   O Abilities

3. Illustrate your paragraph. Use the box at the top of this page
   or get a sheet of drawing paper.

"HOW TO"—WRITING DIRECTIONS

Writing directions requires your students to think carefully about the sequence in which something occurs.

The best way to begin is to have the children tell you the steps in doing a common activity such as putting on a jacket, making a sandwich, going to the drinking fountain, etc. It is especially helpful if you do each step as they describe it. After several oral activities, assign the worksheets provided in this section.

Tell Me How and **How Would You . . .** each require the students to list the steps in doing an activity—either a common one they do every day (brushing teeth) or one requiring the use of imagination (capturing an elephant).

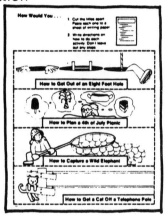

Treasure Hunt and **From Here to There** have students give directions on how to get from a starting point to a final goal.

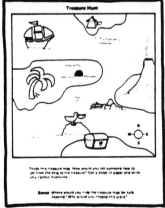
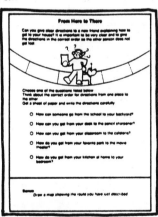

"Witch's Brew" and **"Super Stuff"** allow students to create unusual recipes. They then write a paragraph explaining the results of using the strange concoctions!

55

1. Cut the titles apart. Paste each one to a sheet of writing paper.

2. Write directions on how to do each activity. Don't leave out any steps.

Tell Me How

How to Change a Light Bulb

How to Brush Your Teeth

How to Polish Your Shoes

How to Make _____
(your favorite dessert)

How Would You . . .

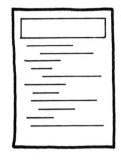

1. Cut the titles apart. Paste each one to a sheet of writing paper.

2. Write directions on how to do each activity. Don't leave out any steps.

How to Get Out of an Eight Foot Hole

How to Plan a 4th of July Picnic

How to Capture a Wild Elephant

How to Get a Cat Off a Telephone Pole

Treasure Hunt

Study this treasure map. How would you tell someone how to get from the ship to the treasure? Get a sheet of paper and write very careful directions.

Bonus: *Where would you hide the treasure map for safe keeping? Why would you choose this place?*

From Here to There

Can you give clear directions to a new friend explaining how to get to your house? It is important to be very clear and to give the directions in the correct order so the other person does not get lost.

Choose one of the questions listed below.
Think about the correct order for directions from one place to the other.
Get a sheet of paper and write the directions carefully.

○ How can someone go from the school to your backyard?

○ How can you get from your desk to the pencil sharpener?

○ How can you get from your classroom to the cafeteria?

○ How do you get from your favorite park to the movie theater?

○ How do you get from your kitchen at home to your bedroom?

Bonus:
    Draw a map showing the route you have just described.

What will you put in this brew?

_____   _____

_____   _____

_____   _____

Now how are you going to use this special brew?

_____

_____

_____

_____

_____

_____

_____

_____

Turn this paper over. Draw a picture showing how
someone would look after using your "Witch's Brew."

"Super Stuff"—the Drink of Champions

Before drinking
"Super Stuff"

Ingredients:

_____

_____

_____

_____

_____

_____

_____

After drinking
"Super Stuff"

How to prepare "Super Stuff":

1. _____

_____

2. _____

_____

3. _____

_____

4. _____

_____

LETTER WRITING

This section allows students to practice letter writing as they use their imaginations.

You will find a page in this section that can be used as a form on which to write or as a template with a sheet of typing or ditto paper.

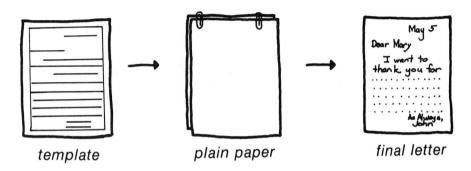

template   plain paper   final letter

Three writing activities are provided in this section:

Write a Fictional Character
Write an Alien Pen Pal
Write the President of the United States

Review the correct form of a friendly letter.
Brainstorm before each writing lesson. Here are some questions you might use:

> *Who are you going to write?*
>
> *What are you going to tell this person or character?*
>
> *What do you want to ask this person or character?*

You may use the completed letters for an additional writing activity. Pass the letters out to other students. They pretend to be the person or character to whom the letter was written and answer the questions asked in the letter.

You may also wish to have your students practice addressing envelopes. Use either real envelopes or have the children fold a sheet of paper into the appropriate shape.

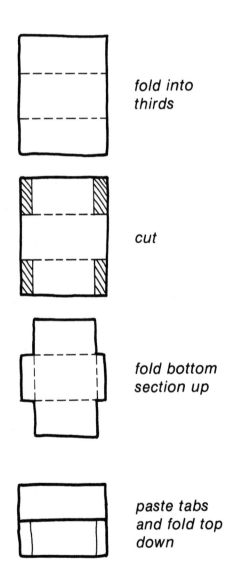

fold into thirds

cut

fold bottom section up

paste tabs and fold top down

_____

Date

_____,

Greeting

_____

Body of letter

_____

_____

_____

_____

_____

_____

_____

_____

_____

_____,

Closing

_____

Signature

Write a Fairy Tale Character

_____
date

Dear _____,
name of character

I just read about you in the story _____
name of story

_____ . I enjoyed the story. The best

part was when _____

_____

_____

There are some things I would like to know. Will you please write me
back and answer these questions?

_____

_____

_____

_____

_____

Sincerely,

_____
write your name here

Bonus: Get a sheet of paper. Pretend you are the character you just
wrote. Write a letter back to yourself answering the questions in
the letter.

Turn your imagination to the stars. Is there anyone out there? Suppose one day you went to the maibox and took out a letter from a far out planet. What do you think the letter would say?

- *Think* about a name for your alien pen pal. Decide where this new friend lives. Decide what you think the letter might tell you about life on the alien planet. The letter might tell you:

    - what the strange pen pal looks like
    - what the planet looks like
    - all about his/her family
    - what kinds of pets they have
    - the games they play
    - their hobbies

- The letter might ask you:

    What do you look like?
    What does Earth look like?
    Tell about your family.
    What kinds of pets and games do Earthlings have?

- Now write the letter. *Remember* you are pretending to be the alien. Don't forget to include:

    Date
    Greeting—Dear *put your name in the greeting*
    Indent the first sentence of each paragraph in the body of the letter.
    Closing
    Signature—*put the alien's name here*

Bonus: include a picture of the alien or of his/her planet with the letter

---

Dear Mr. President

Here is your chance to let the President know how you feel.

Think about what you would like to say in your letter.

Do you have a concern about something you want to tell him about?

Is there something you think needs to be changed?

Do you want to let him know you think he is doing a good job in some area?

Do you want to ask him some questions about what being President is like?

Do you want to ask anything about how you prepare for such a difficult position?

Do you want to ask about his family?

Do you want to know about his life when he was your age?

When you know what you are going to say to the President, get a sheet of paper and write your letter.

Write using your best handwriting. Remember to include:

> Date
> Greeting
> Indent the first sentence of each paragraph of the body of the letter.
> Closing
> Your signature

Address your letter to: President _____
                                 The White House
                                 1600 Pennsylvania Ave.
                                 Washington, D.C. 20006

Seasonal Cinquain

Select a topic:

Fall	Winter	Spring
leaves	rain	flowers
harvest	cold	kites
friends	snow	butterfly
yourself	mitten	clouds
Halloween	Christmas	Easter

Discuss possible words and ideas to use. Write these on the chalkboard for future reference.

Review the steps in writing cinquain.

> Line 1: one word *(title)*
> Line 2: two words *(describe the title)*
> Line 3: three words *(describe an action)*
> Line 4: four words *(describe a feeling)*
> Line 5: one word *(refer back to the title)*

Take the time to write several cinquain verses as a group activity before assigning it as independent work.

A Cinquain

1. Choose a topic 2. Write a cinquain 3. Illustrate your poem

One Word
(title)

Two Words
(describe title)

Three Words
(describe an action)

Four Words
(express a feeling)

One Word
(refer back to title)

Students write using the form provided or on a sheet of writing paper.

Haiku

Review the form of a haiku poem.

Three lines containing 17 syllables which usually refer to nature or the season.

Line 1: 5 syllables
Line 2: 7 syllables
Line 3: 5 syllables

Read samples from the old masters to your students to help them understand the pattern involved.

Write several haiku poems together; then assign haiku as an independent activity.

Students should start with the thought and then try to make the syllable count fit.

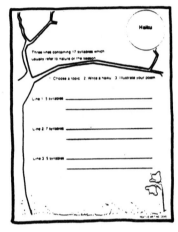

Students write on the form provided or on any type of writing paper.

Shape Poem

Student selects an object. Simple shapes work best.

They draw the basic outline of the shape using black crayon or pen.

Discuss descriptive words and phrases about the object.

Select the best ones and arrange them so they have a pleasing sound.

The student places a sheet of plain paper (ditto or typing) over the drawing. Fasten the pages together with a paper clip.

Then the child writes the phrases following the shape of the object to create the "shape poem."

Remove the top sheet and glue to colored paper to create a frame.

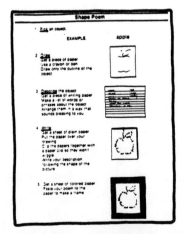

Couplets

A couplet is two lines that rhyme. In this activity the children will use a name as the first line of the couplet. Choose a name. (your own, teacher, friend, someone from history, a story character, someone in the news) The student must then think of words that rhyme with the chosen name. A sentence about the person is then created using one of the rhyming words.

> Jacques Cousteau
> Sails to and fro!

> Mrs. Anne Sneed
> Taught me to read.

A series of couplets can be created to form a longer verse.

The Name Game

1. Choose a name.

   EXAMPLE:
   SARAH LANE

2. Make a list of words that rhyme with the name.

stain	crane
plane	Jane
brain	Maine
detain	explain

3. Write the verse.

   Line 1: Name
   Line 2: A rhyming sentence about the person.

   SARAH LANE
   Lived in Maine
   or
   SARAH LANE
   What a brain
   or
   SARAH LANE
   Flies a plane

   You can try the Name Game here.

   Try several different ones.

> Sarah Lane
> Lived in Maine
>
> Now she's in L.A.
> And plans to stay.

Alphabet Poems

This activity can lead to diligent use of a dictionary or thesaurus. Students select a word. Then think of words that describe it or its actions.

The word selected is written vertically:

Cruises
Along
Roadway

Wriggle
Over
Roots
Munching
Soil

The describing sentence is written horizontally using each letter to begin a word.

Alphabet Poems

1. Choose a word.

   EXAMPLE:
   worms

2. Think of as many words as you can that describe the word you picked. They must all begin with one of the letters in the word you chose.

wriggle	wriggle	wet
obstacle	over	outside
many	move	munch
slippery	smooth	soil
reddish	roots	rocks

   You can write one here.

3. Write your word down the paper. Make the letters dark.

   W
   O
   R
   M
   S

4. Pick some words from your list. Use them to make a sentence. Write the words across from the letters.

   Wriggle
   Over
   Roots
   Munching
   Soil

Limericks

Limericks follow an AABBA rhyming pattern, with the last line rhyming with the first two. Read some of the works of Edward Lear to show children the rhyming pattern.

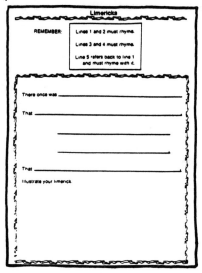

It is very helpful to practice first by providing part of the rhyme, with the class providing the rest.

THERE ONCE WAS A CAT NAMED SAM
WHO ALWAYS WAS CAUGHT IN A JAM

_____

_____

THAT MISCHEVIOUS CAT NAMED SAM.

Making lists of rhyming words on the chalkboard can help students who are having difficulty.

A Cinquain

1. Choose a topic   2. Write a cinquain   3. Illustrate your poem

One Word
(title) _____

Two Words
(describe title) _____

Three Words
(describe an action) _____

Four Words
(express a feeling) _____

One Word
(refer back to title) _____

Shape Poem

1. <u>Pick</u> an object.

EXAMPLE: apple

2. <u>Draw</u>:
   Get a piece of paper.
   Use a crayon or pen.
   Draw only the outline of the object.

3. <u>Describe</u> the object:
   Get a piece of writing paper.
   Make a list of words or phrases about the object.
   Arrange them in a way that sounds pleasing to you.

4. <u>Write</u>:
   Get a sheet of plain paper.
   Put the paper over your drawing.
   Clip the papers together with a paper clip so they won't wiggle.
   Write your description following the shape of the picture.

5. Get a sheet of colored paper.
   Paste your poem to the paper to make a frame.

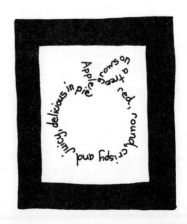

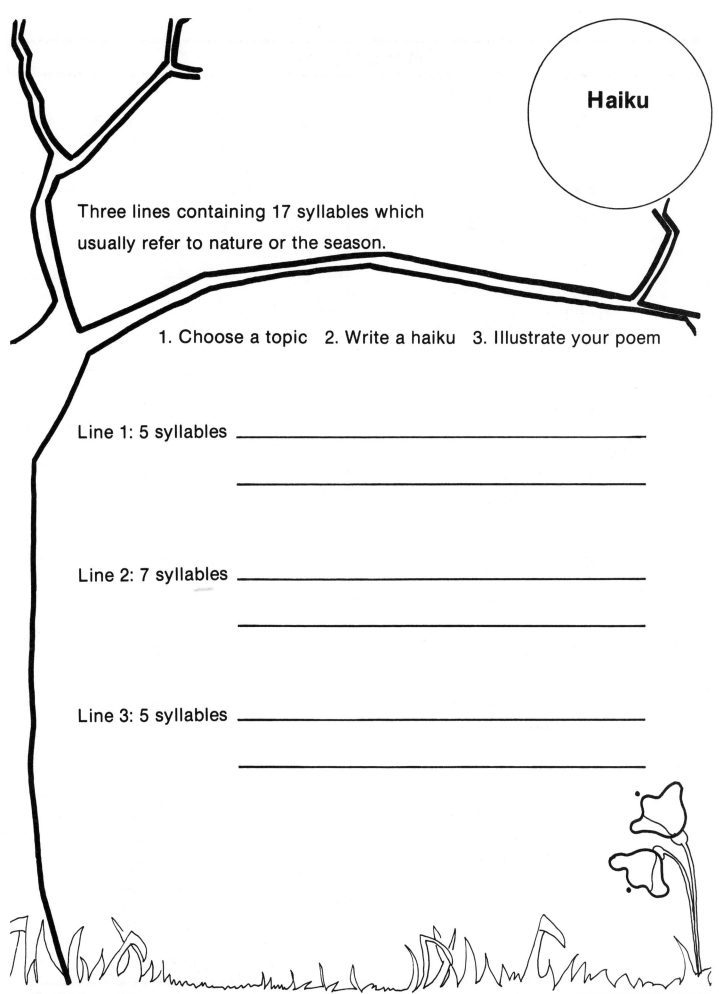

Haiku

Three lines containing 17 syllables which
usually refer to nature or the season.

1. Choose a topic   2. Write a haiku   3. Illustrate your poem

Line 1: 5 syllables _____

_____

Line 2: 7 syllables _____

_____

Line 3: 5 syllables _____

_____

The Name Game

1. Choose a name.

   EXAMPLE:

   SARAH LANE

2. Make a list of words that rhyme with the name.

stain	crane
plane	Jane
brain	Maine
detain	explain

3. Write the verse.


   ```
   Line 1: Name
   Line 2: A rhyming sentence
           about the person.
   ```

   SARAH LANE
   Lived in Maine
   or
   SARAH LANE
   What a brain
   or
   SARAH LANE
   Flies a plane

You can try the Name Game here.

Try several different ones.

Alphabet Poems

1. Choose a word.

   EXAMPLE:

   worms

2. Think of as many words as you can that describe the word you picked. They must all begin with one of the letters in the word you chose.

wriggle	wiggle	wet
obstacle	over	outside
many	move	munch
slippery	smooth	soil
reddish	roots	rocks

3. Write your word down the paper. Make the letters dark.

   W
   O
   R
   M
   S

4. Pick some words from your list. Use them to make a sentence. Write the words across from the letters.

   Wriggle
   Over
   Roots
   Munching
   Soil

You can write one here.

Limericks

REMEMBER:

Lines 1 and 2 must rhyme.

Lines 3 and 4 must rhyme.

Line 5 refers back to line 1 and must rhyme with it.

There once was _____

That _____ .

_____

_____ .

That _____ .

Illustrate your limerick.